Having a Picnic

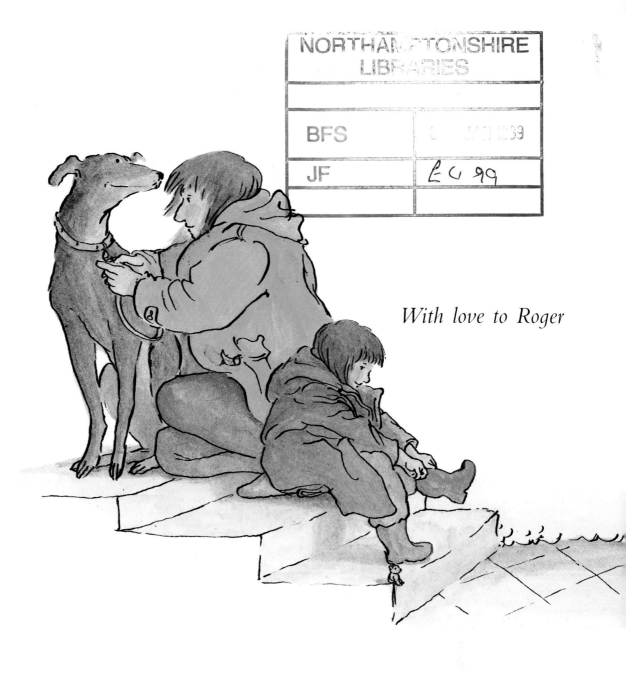

With love to Roger

SARAH GARLAND

Having a Picnic

PUFFIN BOOKS

Off for a picnic.

Into the park.

Up the hill. . .

to look at the view.

Down to the pond. . .

to feed the ducks.

Where's the picnic?

Here it is!

Who's this?

Look out!

They've taken the buns!

Have a good picnic!

PUFFIN BOOKS

Published by the Penguin Group
Penguin Books Ltd, 27 Wrights Lane, London W8 5TZ, England
Penguin Books USA Inc., 375 Hudson Street, New York, New York 10014, USA
Penguin Books Australia Ltd, Ringwood, Victoria, Australia
Penguin Books Canada Ltd, 10 Alcorn Avenue, Toronto, Ontario, Canada M4V 3B2
Penguin Books (NZ) Ltd, 182–190 Wairau Road, Auckland 10, New Zealand

Penguin Books Ltd, Registered Offices: Harmondsworth, Middlesex, England

First published by The Bodley Head 1984
Published in Picture Puffins 1986
Reissued in Puffin Books 1995
3 5 7 9 10 8 6 4

Copyright © Sarah Garland, 1984
All rights reserved

Made and printed in Italy by Printers srl – Trento